theToddler Journey

The Toddler Journey: 100 Hands-On Activities to Keep Your Toddler Busy, Learning, & Growing

All contents copyright © 2016 by Angela Thayer

TeachingMama.org

ISBN-13: 978-1532949449

ISBN-10: 1532949448

Publishing and Design Services | MelindaMartin.me

Disclaimer: All activities are designed to be completed with adult supervision. Please use your judgment when setting up these activities for your child. I do not take responsibility for the safety of these activities. Know your child and your child's nature before trying these. If your toddler still puts items in his or her mouth, you will want to avoid activities with small parts. Always be within arm's reach when doing these activities.

the Toddler Journey

100 Hands-On Activities to Keep Your Toddler Busy, Learning, & Growing

Angela Thayer

CONTENTS

INTRODUCTION

The toddler years are an amazing journey. These years are filled with so much growth, and believe it or not, the time goes by very quickly! The brain develops most rapidly between birth and age 5, which makes the toddler years a pivotal time in a child's life. While it's not necessary to do formal learning activities with toddlers, they learn an incredible amount through play activities. *The Toddler Journey* explores the toddler age and gives you the tools you need to make the most of the toddler years.

The Toddler Journey is full of information and activities to keep your little ones busy, learning, and growing. This book is designed to give parents and childcare providers an understanding of how toddlers develop and also ideas to keep toddlers busy. Toddlers aren't very independent and need constant attention; this book will help you plan your day and help your little one thrive during these important years.

So why do I call this book *The Toddler Journey*? The word "journey" means traveling from one place to another, and often takes a rather long time! The toddler years are a journey, and some days it may seem like a very long one. Developmental milestones don't always happen overnight, and may take lots of practice for skills to develop. When your child is in preschool and beyond, you'll look back and realize how quickly the toddler years went by!

This book is your ultimate guide for helping your child thrive and grow during the toddler years. In the first section of the book, I share developmental milestones for toddlers. I collaborated with Heather Greutman, a Certified Occupational Therapist Assistant and blogger at Growing Hands-On Kids, to put this list together.

Next, I share 100 activities for toddlers in the areas of sensory play, gross motor, fine motor, art, and mess-free activities. These activities give you ideas to not only keep toddlers busy, but to work on developmental milestones.

This book is jam-packed with resources and activities that can help you keep your sanity during the toddler years! I can't wait to dive in!

DEVELOPMENTAL MILESTONES FOR TODDLERS

It's important to know what types of activities are both developmentally and age appropriate for your child. Just remember that the ages and skills listed are not set in stone and that each child is different. This list is for educational and general information purposes only and should not be used to diagnose any type of developmental delay. If you suspect your toddler is delayed in any area, please consult with your pediatrician.

12-18 MONTHS

Gross Motor Development

- stands without support
- begins to walk
- crawls on furniture
- starts, stops, and turns without falling
- begins to run
- squats down to pick something up

- begins to crawl up the stairs and creep back down
- sits down in a chair independently
- pulls a toy behind them while walking
- throws a ball underhand while sitting
- carries a large toy without falling

Fine Motor Development

- builds a tower 2 blocks high
- claps hands together
- waves goodbye
- scoops objects with a spoon or small shovel

- bangs objects together using both hands
- puts small objects into a container
- scribbles with crayons on paper

Speech & Language Development

- uses one to two words meaningfully
- says "mama" and "dada" and exclamations like "uh-oh"
- begins to copy words
- babbles as if having a real conversation

- practices speech sounds such as raising tone when asking a question
- uses arms and fingers to point items they want
- starts to make many common consonant sounds, such as t,d,n,w, and h

Social & Emotional Development

- shows possible shyness or nervousness
- cries when mom or dad leaves
- has favorite items or people
- shows fear in some situations
- hands you a book when they want to hear a story

- repeats sounds or actions to get attention
- puts out an arm or leg to help with dressing
- plays games such a "peek-a-boo" and "pat-a-cake"

Cognitive Development

- explores things in different ways, like shaking, banging, and throwing
- finds hidden objects easily
- looks at the correct picture or object when it is named

- copies gestures
- starts to use items correctly, e.g. drinking from a cup
- follows simple directions like "pick up that toy"

18-24 MONTHS

Gross Motor Development

- jumps with feet together, clearing the floor
- squats down to play ✔
- walks up and down the stairs ✔
- stands on tiptoes with support ✔
- starts to use riding toys ✔
- throws a ball into a box ✔
- kicks a ball forwards ✔

Fine Motor Development

- puts rings on pegs ✔
- begins holding a crayon with finger tips and thumb ✔
- removes pegs from a pegboard ✔
- marks or scribbles with a crayon or pencil ✔
- builds a tower 3-4 blocks high ✔
- opens loosely wrapped packages or containers ✔
- starts to cut paper with scissors (closer to 2 years old) ✔
- turns pages in a book one page at a time ✔

Speech & Language Development

- says and shakes head "no" ✔
- understands simple commands and questions ✔
- starts stringing two words together ✔
- begins to name objects around them ✔
- overextends words they already know: ie. all new animals may be called "dog" ✔
- points to objects they want ✔

Social & Emotional Development

- likes to hands things to others as play ✔
- has possible temper tantrums ✔
- has possible fear of strangers ✔
- shows affection to familiar people ✔
- plays simple pretend play, such as feeding dolls ✔
- clings to caregivers in new situations. ✔
- explores alone but with parent close by ✔

Cognitive Development

- knows what ordinary objects are: ie. telephone, brush, spoon, etc. ✔
- points to get the attention of others
- shows interest in dolls or stuffed animals and pretends to feed them ✔
- points to one body part when it is named ✔
- follows one-step verbal commands without any gestures: ie. "sit down" ✔

24-36 MONTHS

Gross Motor Development

- stands on tiptoes
- jumps from the bottom step
- rides a tricycle with feet on the floor (24-30 months)
- rides a tricycle with feet on the pedals (30-36 months)
- stands on a balance beam with two feet and walks forward
- catches a large ball with hands straight out and arms bent (30-36 months)
- stands on one foot momentarily (up to 5 seconds)
- walks up the stairs while alternating feet
- walks heal-to-toe in a straight line
- jumps over a small stationery object

Fine Motor Development

(2 years old)

- manipulates clay or play dough
- stacks a block tower 9 blocks high
- turns doorknobs
- picks up small objects with pincer grasp (index finger and thumb)
- completes 3-piece puzzles
- scribbles on paper
- makes snips on paper with scissors
- washes hands independently
- screws lids on containers on and off
- strings large beads
- zips and unzips large zippers
- uses a spoon correctly

(3 years old)

- draws a circle after being shown how
- cuts a piece of paper in half
- copies pre-written lines of vertical, horizontal, and circle shapes
- laces a card
- cuts along a wide line with 1/2" accuracy
- strings 1/2-inch beads
- sorts objects
- fastens and unfastens large buttons

Speech & Language Development

- begins to experiment with sound levels
- says sentences with 2-4 words (age 2)
- start to use pronouns in speech
- follows simple directions
- points to items in a book
- knows around 200 words (by age 3)
- begins to use past tense and plurals
- starts to answer simple questions
- speaks understandably (by age 3)
- carries on a sustained conversation

24-36 MONTHS (CONT.)

Social & Emotional Development

Before age 3

- copies others, especially other adults and other children
- gets excited when with other children
- shows more independence
- shows defiant behavior
- plays mainly beside other children, but begins to include other children in play

By age 3:

- shows affection for friends without prompting
- takes turns in games
- shows concern for crying friend or family member
- understands the idea of "mine" and "his" or "hers"
- shows a wide range of emotions
- separates easily from mom and dad
- gets upset with major changes in routine
- dresses and undresses self

Cognitive Development

Before age 3

- begins to sort shapes and colors
- completes sentences and rhymes in familiar books
- plays simple make-believe games
- uses one hand more than the other
- follows two-step instructions
- names items in a picture book

By age 3:

- works toys with buttons, levers, and moving parts
- plays make-believe with dolls, animals and people
- does puzzles with 3 or 4 pieces
- understands what "two" means

Sensory Play

You've probably heard of sensory play, but did you know that this type of play is very beneficial for children? From birth, babies learn about their world using their senses, such as seeing, smelling, hearing, feeling & tasting. As they grow, children's senses are their most familiar and most basic way to explore and process new information. Sensory play enhances learning through hands-on activities that stimulate the child's senses. This is a great way for children to explore the world they live in!

Research tells us that sensory play has many benefits. Here are a few:

- Builds nerve connections in the brain's pathways, which leads to the child's ability to complete more complex learning tasks

- Sends signals to the child's brain that helps strengthen neural pathways important for all types of learning

- Supports language development, cognitive growth, fine & gross motor skills, problem solving, and social interaction

- Helps develop and enhance memory

- Calms children who may be anxious or frustrated

- Helps children learn sensory attributes (ex: hot, cold, dry, wet, hard, soft)

- Invites children to be creative and imaginative

Toddlers learn a tremendous amount through play. Yes, sensory play can be messy, but embracing the mess and watching your toddler learn through play is priceless.

In this section, I share 25 hands-on activities that will engage your toddler's senses. All of the activities use just a few ingredients, but lead to hours of play!

SOAP FOAM

SENSORY

Materials Needed

- 2 tablespoons of dish soap
- 1/4 cup of water
- food coloring
- food processor or blender
- large plastic bin

Ways to Play

- Scoop up the soft, silky, fluffy soap foam in your hands.
- Use spoons or cups to scoop it up and play with it.

Pre-Activity Prep

Place the dish soap, water, and a few drops of food coloring inside of the food processor or blender. Blend for a minute or two (until the soap foam rises to the top). Scoop out the soap foam and put it into a large container. Repeat the recipe to make more colors.

Other Notes

The soap foam stays fluffy for about 15 minutes, so make sure to use the soap foam right away. If the foam starts to get flat, put it back in the blender and mix for another minute.

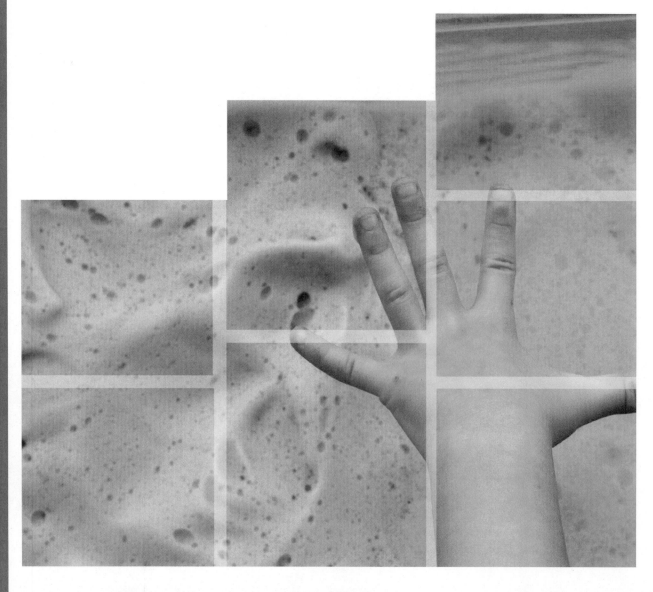

Materials Needed

- large plastic bin
- containers: plastic pitchers, cups, measuring cups, etc.
- food coloring (optional)
- water

Ways to Play

- Pour water into other containers or inside the bin.
- Mix the colored water together.

Pre-Activity Prep

Pour water into a bin. If you want your child to play with colored water, add water to some containers and a few drops of food coloring.

Other Notes

This is a great way to also practice a life skill with toddlers. They will most likely spill water when pouring from a pitcher initially, but with practice, they will improve!

SENSORY

CLOUD DOUGH

12-18 18-24 24-36

Materials Needed

- 8 cups of flour
- 1 cup of vegetable oil
- plastic bin

Pre-Activity Prep

Combine the flour with the oil. Mix together with your hands for 3-5 minutes, or until the dough starts sticking together. The dough is ready when you can make it into a ball.

Ways to Play

- Scoop it up in your hands and mold it into balls.
- Pour cloud dough into a cup and pack it down. Tip the cup over to get it out and you have a neat mold!
- Make a road with the dough and drive vehicles on it.
- You can also add in ½ cup of cocoa powder to the recipe to make it smell like chocolate.

Other Notes

The cloud dough will last indefinitely when stored in a container with a lid.

SENSORY

12-18 **18-24** **24-36**

Materials Needed

- 1 can of shaving cream
- food coloring
- muffin tin
- paintbrushes

Ways to Play

- Use paintbrushes or fingers to paint designs around the bathtub.
- Feel the foamy bath paint in your hands.

Pre-Activity Prep

Spray shaving cream into the muffin tin. Squirt a drop of food coloring into each section. Stir to mix up the color.

Other Notes

When finished with the bath paint, simply wipe down the walls of the tub with a damp rag.

Please make sure to not use gel food coloring. This can stain skin and the bathtub.

SENSORY

SOUND BASKET

Materials Needed

- basket
- items that make sounds: egg shakers, small pot with lid, stick, tambourine, whistle, etc.
- homemade items: water bottle or plastic egg with rice or dry corn inside, empty canister for a drum, etc.

Ways to Play

- Explore and listen to the sounds made from the instruments.
- Create different rhythms with the instruments.
- Try playing two instruments at the same time to work on coordination.

Pre-Activity Prep

Prepare the homemade instruments. Place all the items in a basket.

SENSORY

14

Materials Needed

- 5 cups of fine sand
- 3 teaspoons of tempera powder paint (or a few drops of food coloring)
- 1.5 cups of corn starch
- 1/2 teaspoon of Dawn dish soap
- 1 cup of water
- large plastic bin

Ways to Play

- Dig your hands into the bin and have fun molding the dough into balls or other shapes.
- Hide plastic gold coins or other objects in the rainbow sand and have the child search for them.

Other Notes

I do not recommend using this activity if your child still puts items in his or her mouth.

After playing with the moldable sand, store in an air-tight container. The sand may become a little dry, so spritz in some water to make it moist again.

Pre-Activity Prep

Combine the sand with the tempera paint. Mix in the corn starch. Then mix in the dish soap with the water and slowly pour it over the sand mixture. The sand should feel slightly wet and you should be able to easily mold it into shapes. If it feels too dry, add in some more water. Repeat these steps to make each color.

SENSORY

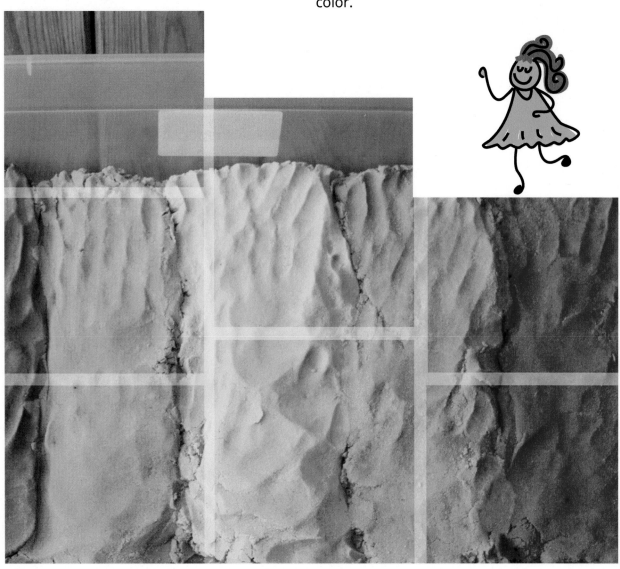

SENSORY

Materials Needed

- plastic bin
- large tapioca pearls (the ones that are used for bubble tea and cook in 5 minutes)
- gel food coloring

Ways to Play

- Scoop them up in your hands or in containers.
- Pour them through funnels.
- Squish the beads.
- Sort them by colors.

Pre-Activity Prep

Boil 10 cups of water for 1 cup of pearls. Once the water is boiling, add the tapioca. After one minute they will rise to the top. Stir them and put the lid on. Let them sit for 4 more minutes. Drain and rinse them with cold water.

If you want the tapioca pearls to be colored, follow these instructions:

Separate them into bowls for different colors. Use gel food coloring to dye the clear ones and to make the colored tapioca pearls brighter. To let the color soak in, lay them on wax paper and let them sit for an hour to dry.

Place the water beads in a plastic bin and add a little bit of water to it, since they tend to get sticky.

Other Notes

1. These are safe to eat, but I would not encourage your child to eat them.
2. The food coloring does wear off slightly in the water and on hands.
3. These do not last long. They start turning mushy after 1 day.

Materials Needed

- tray
- shaving cream
- items to put in the shaving cream: water beads, blocks, plastic animals, etc.

Ways to Play

- Mix in food coloring to change the color of the shaving cream.
- Add in water beads for exploring a different texture.
- Put in plastic animal figurines for dramatic play.

Pre-Activity Prep

Spray shaving cream onto a tray.

Other Notes

Make sure to watch toddlers carefully so they don't put the cream in their mouths. If you are concerned about this, use whipped cream instead.

S E N S O R Y

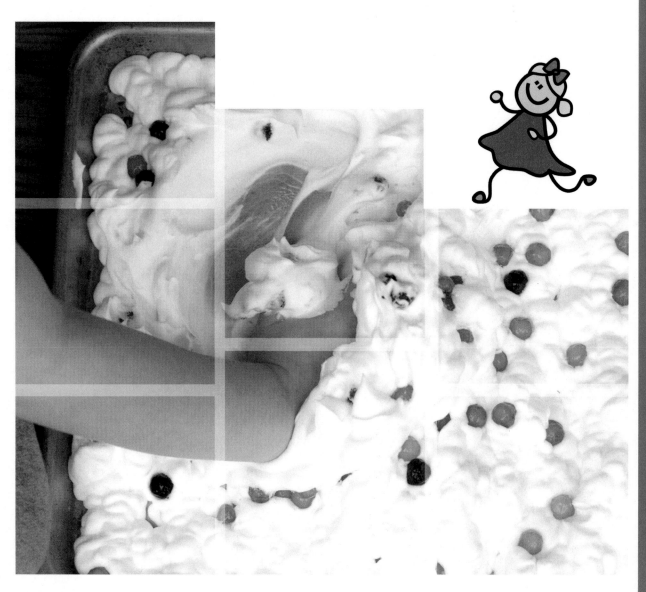

PASTA SENSORY BIN

Materials Needed

- 2 cups dry pasta
- 1/4 cup rubbing alcohol
- food coloring
- wax paper
- gallon-size plastic bags
- items to play with the sensory bin

Ways to Play

- Scoop or pour the noodles into containers.
- Use tongs to pick up the noodles.
- Sort the pasta by colors.
- Thread the pasta on yarn to make necklaces.

Pre-Activity Prep

Pour the pasta into a Ziploc bag and pour rubbing alcohol into the bag. Add the food coloring to the bag. Close the bag and shake until all the noodles are colored. Let the pasta sit in the bag for 5-7 minutes. Spread the noodles out on wax paper. Let them dry for a couple of hours. Once they are dry, pour the noodles into a plastic bin. Repeat this to make more colors.

Other Notes

The noodles will last indefinitely. Store them in a Ziploc bag or plastic container.

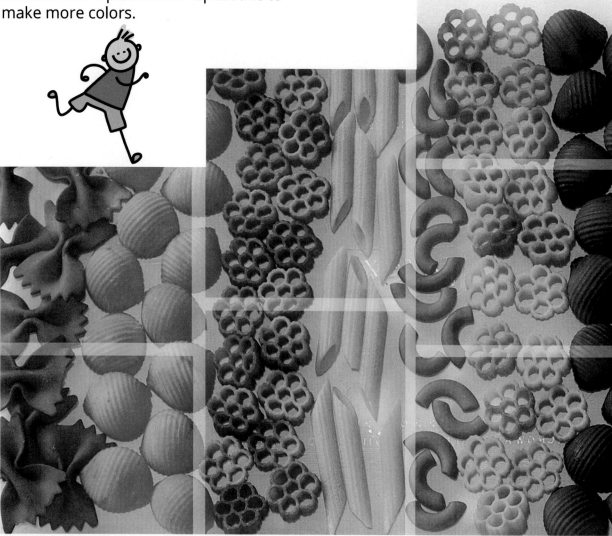

SENSORY

18

Materials Needed

- empty plastic wipes container
- various strips of ribbon or fabric

Ways to Play

- Put your hand inside the container and pull out the ribbons.
- Explore the different textures of the ribbons.
- Stuff the ribbons back into the container.

Pre-Activity Prep

Cut pieces of ribbon or fabric into strips about 12 inches long. Place them inside of an empty plastic wipes container.

S E N S O R Y

POOL NOODLE BATH

SENSORY

Materials Needed

- pool noodles
- serrated knife
- bath tub

Pre-Activity Prep

Cut a pool noodle into pieces using a knife. Place the pieces into a bathtub filled with water for the child to play with.

Ways to Play

- Stick the pool noodles to the sides of the bath tub.
- Stack them in a tower.
- Count or sort them.
- Draw a picture on 1 pool noodle piece and place it face down in the tub. Have your toddler search for it by flipping them over until he finds it.

Other Notes

Dry the pool noodle pieces and store them in a bag to use again.

Materials Needed

- plastic bin
- boxes of Jell-O

Pre-Activity Prep

Make the Jell-O according to the directions on the box.

You can do this activity two different ways:

1. Cut the Jell-O into squares and place them into a bin for the child to play with.
2. Place plastic figurines into the Jell-O before putting it in the refrigerator.

Ways to Play

- Explore the Jell-O with hands, scoopers, tongs, lemon squeezers, or kid tweezers.
- If the Jell-O has items inside, dig in the Jell-O and pull them out.
- Talk about how the Jell-O feels. Does it feel cold? Squishy? Sticky? What does it smell like? Or taste like?

Other Notes

This sensory activity is a one-time activity. Please dispose of it after the activity is done.

SENSORY

erials Needed

- cold water
- flour
- f boiling water
- oring

Ways to Play

- Use hands to paint and create designs on paper.
- If a child is apprehensive about using their hands, start with a paintbrush.

Activity Prep

of cold water and 1 cup of
pan on the stove. Gradually
of boiling water to the mix.
eat until it boils. Take off the
t it cool. Then divide the mix-
owls and add food coloring.

Other Notes

This finger paint can be kept in an air-tight container in the refrigerator for a few weeks.

Materials Needed

- plastic bin
- boxes of Jell-O

Pre-Activity Prep

Make the Jell-O according to the directions on the box.

You can do this activity two different ways:

1. Cut the Jell-O into squares and place them into a bin for the child to play with.
2. Place plastic figurines into the Jell-O before putting it in the refrigerator.

Ways to Play

- Explore the Jell-O with hands, scoopers, tongs, lemon squeezers, or kid tweezers.
- If the Jell-O has items inside, dig in the Jell-O and pull them out.
- Talk about how the Jell-O feels. Does it feel cold? Squishy? Sticky? What does it smell like? Or taste like?

Other Notes

This sensory activity is a one-time activity. Please dispose of it after the activity is done.

SENSORY

EDIBLE FINGER PAINT

Materials Needed

- 1 cup of cold water
- 1 cup of flour
- 3 cups of boiling water
- food coloring
- bowls

Ways to Play

- Use hands to paint and create designs on paper.
- If a child is apprehensive about using their hands, start with a paintbrush.

Pre-Activity Prep

Pour 1 cup of cold water and 1 cup of flour into a pan on the stove. Gradually add 3 cups of boiling water to the mix. Stir over heat until it boils. Take off the heat and let it cool. Then divide the mixture into bowls and add food coloring.

Other Notes

This finger paint can be kept in an air-tight container in the refrigerator for a few weeks.

SENSORY

SENSORY BOTTLES

Materials Needed

- plastic water bottle
- water or another liquid
- items to put inside the water bottle
- hot glue gun

Pre-Activity Prep

There are lots of ways to make sensory bottles. A sensory bottle is filled with eye-catching items for a child to look at. Toddlers love to shake, roll, and watch the items float in the bottle. Once the bottle is ready to go, hot glue the lid down.

Here are five ways to make the bottles:

1. Water, Oil, and Food Coloring
2. 1/4 bottle of clear hand soap, 3/4 bottle of water, beads
3. Water, glitter, sequins
4. Water and rainbow loom bands
5. Colored rice and sequins

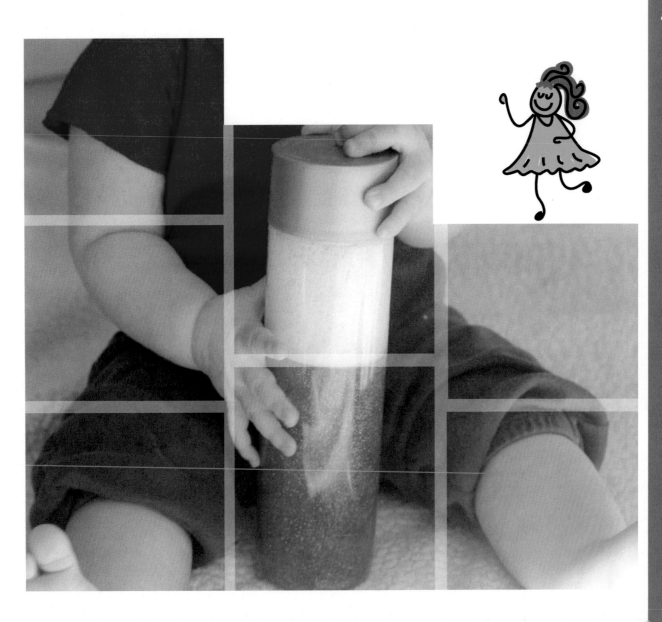

SENSORY

COLORED RICE SENSORY BIN

Materials Needed

- plastic bin
- bag of rice
- 1/4 cup rubbing alcohol
- wax paper
- food coloring
- gallon-sized plastic bags

Ways to Play

- Scoop the rice and pour it into funnels or containers.
- Bury items and try to find them in the rice.

Pre-Activity Prep

Place the rice into a Ziploc gallon-size bag. Then pour about 1/4 cup of rubbing alcohol into the bag (or enough to coat the rice). Close the bag and shake it around. Then drop in some food coloring. Close the bag and shake some more. Let it sit for about 5 minutes. Then spread it out on wax paper and let it dry. Once it's dry, pour the rice in a plastic bin.

Other Notes

The rice will last indefinitely. Store them in a Ziploc bag or plastic container.

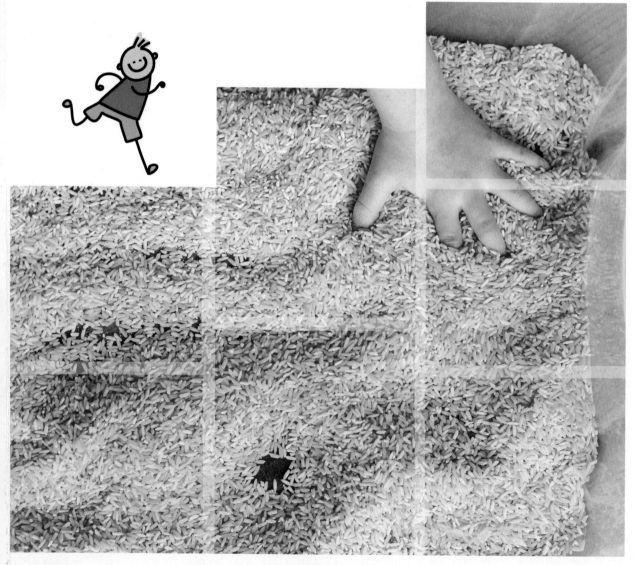

S
E
N
S
O
R
Y

MARSHMALLOW PLAY DOUGH

Materials Needed

- 30 large marshmallows
- 1 tablespoon of coconut oil
- about 2 cups of cornstarch
- food coloring

Ways to Play

- Mold into shapes like balls or snakes to work on hand strength.
- Pull and twist the soft and bendy dough.
- Use kid scissors to cut the dough.

Other Notes

This sensory activity is a one-time activity. Please dispose of it after the activity is done.

Pre-Activity Prep

Place 1 tablespoon of coconut oil into a pan on medium heat. After it melts, add 30 large marshmallows to the pan. Stir the marshmallows frequently until they are melted. Divide the marshmallow mix into separate bowls if you want more than 1 color. Next, stir in a few drops of food coloring. Then stir in 2 cups of cornstarch and knead it. If it is still sticky, add in some more cornstarch.

SENSORY

25

OATS SENSORY BIN

Materials Needed

- plastic bin
- dry oats
- tools to play with: containers, funnels, scoopers

Ways to Play

- Pick up the oats with scoopers, run them through your hands, pour them into containers, etc.

Other Notes

This is a sensory base material into which you can add other object to play with, such as plastic fruit or toy animals. Oats are great for introducing babies and toddlers to sensory bins. To help with clean up, place a plastic tablecloth underneath the bin and pour the oats back into the bin after play time.

SENSORY

SKITTLES FINGER PAINT

Materials Needed

- 1/2 cup corn starch
- 2 cups water
- 1/2 tsp. salt
- 3 tablespoons sugar
- 1 bag of Skittles

Other Notes

Store the Skittles finger paint in airtight containers. It will last for one week.

Ways to Play

- Use fingers and hands to make designs on paper, trays, or even on a mirror!
- Feel the paint and talk about how it feels, tastes, smells, and looks like.

Pre-Activity Prep

Sort the bag of Skittles by color into bowls (you can have your toddler help with this). Add 1 cup of water to each bowl. Let the Skittles dissolve in the water. After they have dissolved, pour the colored water into a pot. Then add the corn starch, salt, sugar, and 1 more cup of water to the pot. Heat over medium heat and stir frequently. Cook for about 10 minutes. When it starts to thicken, remove from the stove. Don't let it cook for too long or it will be too clumpy. Allow it to cool before letting your child play with it.

SENSORY

CEREAL SENSORY BIN

Materials Needed

- plastic bin
- Cheerios or another cereal

Pre-Activity Prep

Pour the cereal into the plastic bin to play with. Add in other tools, such as tongs, scoopers, and spoons.

Ways to Play

- Scoop up the cereal and pour it into containers.
- Pour cereal into a curved section of a gutter.
- Pour cereal into a funnel over a cup.
- Use a plastic hammer and crunch up the cereal.

SENSORY

Materials Needed

- ice cubes
- bowl of water
- scooper or spoon
- color (optional)

Pre-Activity Prep

Pour ice cubes into a bowl of lukewarm water (you can put a drop of food coloring in if you want color).

Ways to Play

- Transfer ice cubes from the tray to the bowl. The child can choose to use his hands to hold the ice or use a scooper.
- Stir the ice in the bowl of water with a spoon.
- Keep playing with the ice until it's melted.

Other Notes

This is a simple activity that toddlers love. They feel the temperature of the ice, the texture, and it's safe for them to taste the ice! Make sure the ice is not too cold for your little one's fingers.

SENSORY

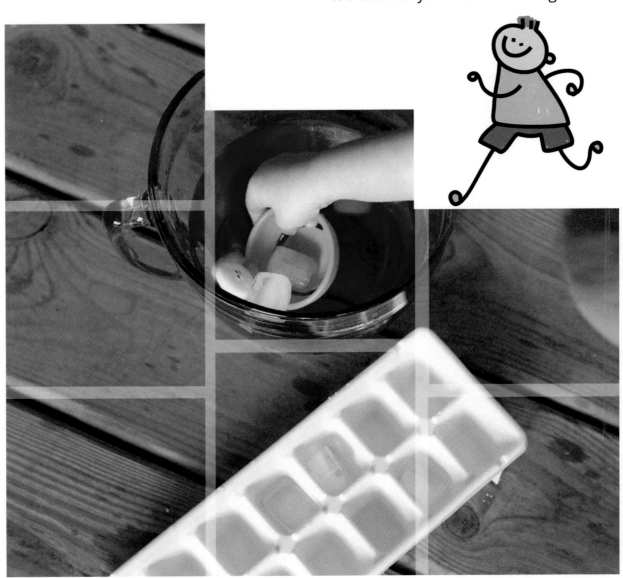

29

RICE CEREAL SENSORY BIN

SENSORY

Materials Needed

- 1 cup baby rice cereal
- 3 tablespoons coconut oil
- plastic tub

Ways to Play

- Touch, smell, or even taste the rice cereal dough.
- Mold and shape the dough together to form a ball or other shapes.
- Talk with your toddler about how the texture feels and smells.

Pre-Activity Prep

Melt the coconut oil over medium heat on the stove. Once it's melted, mix together with 1 cup of rice cereal. Let the mixture cool.

Other Notes

This sensory activity is a one-time activity. Please dispose of it after the activity is done.

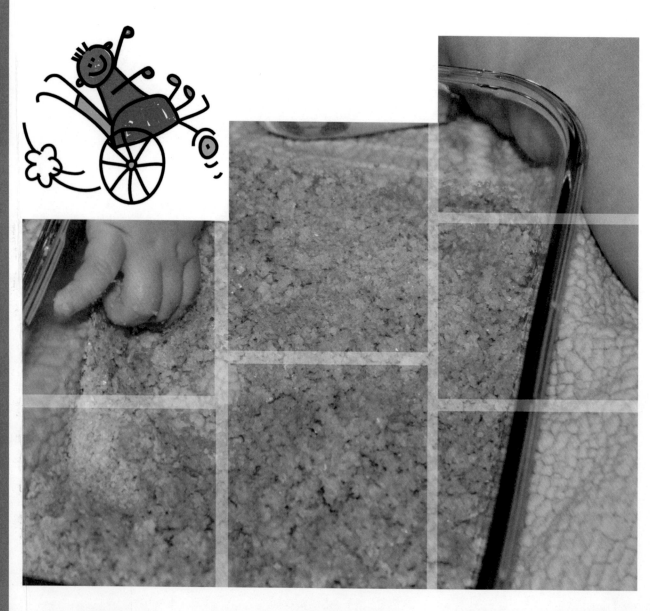

SQUISH BAGS

Materials Needed

- gallon-size Ziploc bags
- liquid for the bag: water, oil, hair gel, etc.
- items to put inside the bag

Pre-Activity Prep

There are so many ways to make squish bags. It's a bag filled with eye-catching items for a child to look at and feel through the bag. They love to touch and squeeze the bag.

Here are a few ways to make the bags:

- water, oil, and food coloring
- hair gel and sequins
- water beads
- hair gel and googly eyes

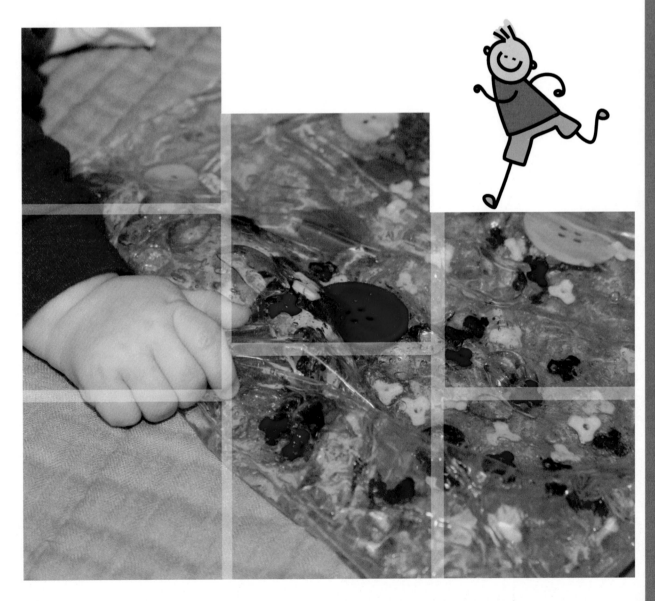

SENSORY

Materials Needed

- 2 tablespoons cornstarch
- 1/4 cup baby soap
- 2 teaspoons water
- 2-3 drops food coloring
- ice cube tray
- paint brush

Ways to Play

- Use paintbrushes or hands to paint designs around the bathtub.

Pre-Activity Prep

Mix the cornstarch with the baby soap. Add water and food coloring. Whisk together and pour them into an ice cube tray. Repeat the recipe to make more colors.

Other Notes

After using the bath paint, rinse it off with a washcloth.

SLIPPERY NOODLES SENSORY BIN

Materials Needed

- spaghetti noodles
- 1 teaspoon olive oil
- Ziploc bags
- tongs
- food coloring

Ways to Play

- Use hands to mix and play with the noodles.
- Fill up cups with the noodles.
- Lift the noodles up with tongs.
- Eat the noodles.

Other Notes

Keep the noodles in the refrigerator inside an airtight container to play with again.

Pre-Activity Prep

Cook the spaghetti noodles according to the package. After draining the water, rinse the noodles with cold water. Mix in the olive oil to keep the noodles from sticking to each other. If you want more than 1 color, separate the noodles into Ziploc bags. Squirt a few drops of food coloring into each bag. Mix with tongs and let it sit in there for 5 minutes. Pour the colored noodles into a bin for your child to play with.

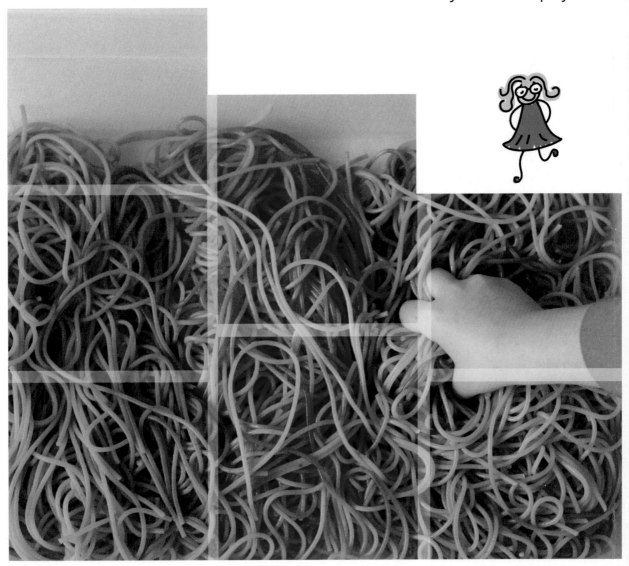

SENSORY

BUBBLE WRAP PAINT BAG

Materials Needed

- bubble wrap
- gallon-sized Ziploc bag
- paint
- tape

Ways to Play

- Feel the paint and bubble wrap through the bag.
- Push the paint together to mix and create new colors.
- Have fun popping the bubble wrap.
- Tape the bag to a window to see how sunlight changes the colors.

Pre-Activity Prep

Cut a piece of bubble wrap to fit into a gallon-sized Ziploc bag. Place it inside the bag and squirt paint into the bag. Seal the bag with tape.

Other Notes

If you're concerned about the bag breaking, you can double-bag it to make it more secure.

SENSORY

Gross Motor Skills

Movement is important to incorporate into every single day, especially with busy toddlers. Gross motor skills are the abilities required to control the large muscles of the body for walking, jumping, skipping, and more.

We learn from head to toe, starting as babies. Our upper body muscle control precedes the lower body muscle control. As babies grow, they first develop control in their trunks and then in their elbows, wrists, and fingers. The same goes for the lower body. Control from the hips is first, then control in the legs, feet, and toes.

Next comes manipulation of toys with fingers and hands. Have you ever noticed that a child contorts their feet or tongue in the early days of drawing with a crayon? It's because they are learning that new skill and it emerges from a near total body involvement.

Lastly, we have the progression of showing preference to one side. For example, kids may start throwing a ball with either hand, but eventually they develop a preference in which hand they use to throw. Children generally experiment with both sides of the body until a preference is made. After they've gained control of their body, they start to build strength.

Gross motor movements are categorized into 3 ways:

1. **Locomotor activity** — movement from one spot to another. Examples: walking, running, climbing, leaping, jumping, hopping, galloping, sliding, and skipping.
2. **Non-locomotor activity** — movement in a stationary place. Examples: pushing, pulling, bending, stretching, twisting, turning, swinging, swaying, rising, and falling.
3. **Manipulative skills** — moving objects in a variety of ways. Examples: throwing, kicking, striking, and catching.

These 25 gross motor activities in this section are easy to implement into your day and will help the child gain strength and confidence in his or her body.

GROSS MOTOR

Materials Needed

- 3 or more hula hoops
- duct tape

Ways to Play

- Crawl through the tunnel of hula hoops.
- Roll a ball through the tunnel.
- Crawl backwards through the hoops.

Pre-Activity Prep

- Place the hula hoops upright and tape them to the floor with duct tape until they stand up on their own. Put 3 or more in a row for the child to crawl through.

Other Notes

Crawling is great for shoulder stability, hand separation, balance, core strength, and body awareness.

Materials Needed

- large piece of bubble wrap
- optional: colored paper or foam sheets

Ways to Play

- Jump on the bubble wrap and enjoy making the popping sounds!
- Say a color and have your toddler jump to the correct color.

Pre-Activity Prep

Lay the bubble wrap on the ground. If you want the child to practice identifying colors, then lay colored sheets underneath the bubble wrap.

GROSS MOTOR

Materials Needed

- stuffed animals
- 2 baskets

Ways to Play

- Pick up stuffed animals from one basket and toss them into the other basket.

Pre-Activity Prep

Gather stuffed animals and place them in a basket. Place another basket a couple feet away.

Other Notes

Tossing is great for working on hand-eye coordination. Toddlers may find tossing stuffed animals easier to handle than a ball because they can't roll away.

GROSS MOTOR

18-24 **24-36**

Materials Needed

- medium-size balls
- empty pop bottles or coffee creamer bottles
- tape

Ways to Play

- Roll the ball down to the bottles and see how many can be knocked down.
- Have your toddler practice setting the "pins" back up after they are knocked down.

Pre-Activity Prep

Set up the bottles on one end of the room. You can start out with just 3 bottles and work up to 10 bottles. Mark the ground with tape to show where the bottles should stand.

GROSS MOTOR

G R O S S M O T O R

Materials Needed

- string or yarn
- chairs

Ways to Play

- Explore the spider web and crawl through it to get to the other side.
- Place a toy in the web and have your child crawl through the web to get it.

Pre-Activity Prep

Take the string and tie one end to a chair and weave it back and forth between the chairs. Keep it low to the ground so your toddler will crawl through the web.

Other Notes

Make sure the child does not get tangled in the web or wrap the string around his or her neck.

Materials Needed

- colored bean bags
- colored foam sheets or paper that matches the bean bag colors

Pre-Activity Prep

Place the colored sheets on the ground.

Ways to Play

- Toss the bean bags onto the colored sheets. Try to match the bean bag to the correct color.
- Use the bean bags to practice positional words. Invite the child to find a bean bag of a specified color and place it in a specified position. For example, "Find the green bean bag and place it in front of the green sheet." Continue with different colored bean bags and different positional words: on, in front, under, near, far, etc.

GROSS MOTOR

41

Materials Needed

- pillows

Pre-Activity Prep

Lay the pillows down on the ground to make an obstacle course.

Ways to Play

- Crawl through the pillows to help your child practice body control.
- Walk on the pillows to work on balance.
- Spread the pillows out with some gap in between and have the child crawl or jump from pillow to pillow.
- Use the pillows to practice positional words. Ask the child to stand on top, beside, behind, in front, near, or far away from the pillows.

G R O S S   M O T O R

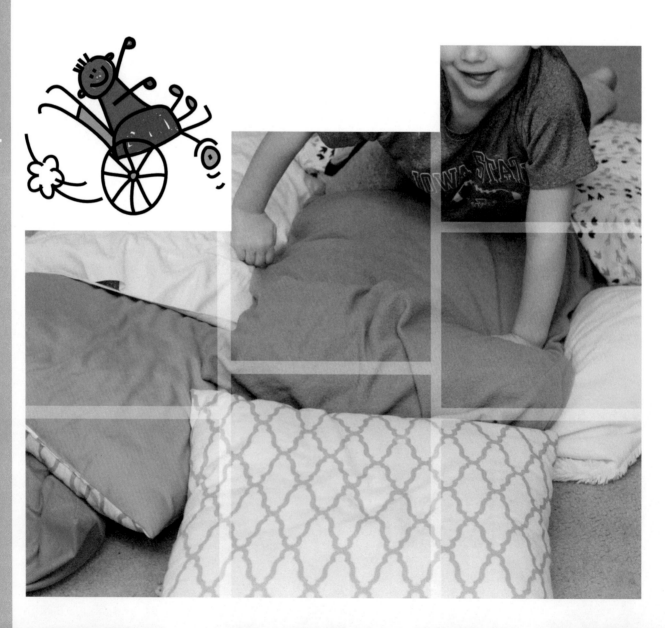

42

Materials Needed

- ball

Ways to Play

- Place the ball between your legs and squeeze your legs together. Waddle around the room like a penguin.
- Jump with the ball between your legs.
- Race with another child or set a timer to see how long your child can hold the ball between their legs.

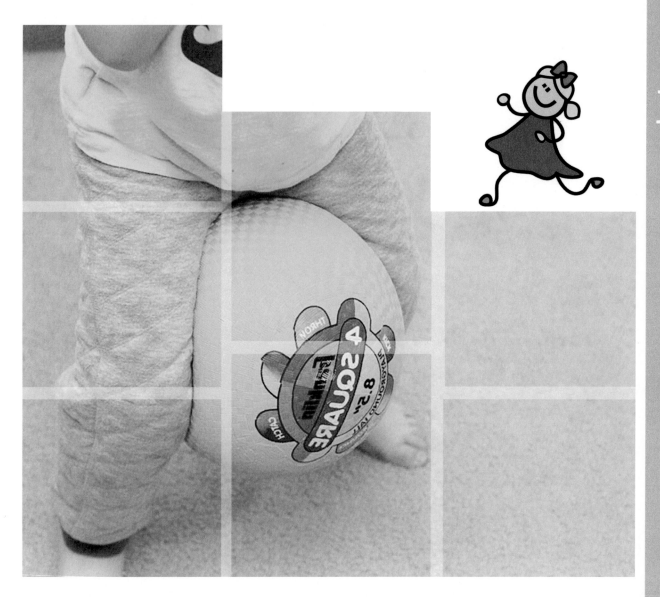

GROSS MOTOR

Materials Needed

- 3 or more hula hoops

Pre-Activity Prep

Place the hula hoops next to each other in a row.

Other Notes

Jumping is a complex skill and takes practice for a child to master it.

Ways to Play

- Jump from one hula hoop to another.
- To make it harder, add space between each hula hoop.
- If a toddler doesn't know how to jump, start with stepping into the hoops. Then teach the child how to leap with one foot and eventually work on jumping with two feet.

Materials Needed

- paper plates

Ways to Play

- Place paper plates underneath your feet and move your feet back and forth in a skating movement.
- Race another child from one side of the room to the other while wearing the paper plate skates.
- Spin around in a circle.

GROSS MOTOR

45

How to Play

Sing the song to your child and have your child do the movement word for the song. When you sing "sun goes down," crouch down to the floor. When you sing "out pops the moon," then jump up.

Movement Song

Tune: Pop Goes the Weasel

Running, running all day long, we like to run to this tune!

But when the sun goes down to sleep then out pops the moon!

Change the action in the song to other words:

- walking
- jumping
- hopping
- skipping
- crawling

Materials Needed

- optional: picture cards of animals

How to Play

- talk with your toddler about how different animals move
- say one of the following animals and have your child act like the animal
- waddle like a penguin
- slither like a snake
- swing like a monkey
- stomp like a dinosaur
- gallop like a horse
- hop like a bunny
- fly like a bird

GROSS MOTOR

Materials Needed

- masking tape or painter's tape

Ways to Play

- Walk on the line of tape.
- Walk backwards, run, jump, walk on toes, etc.
- Place hands on one line and feet on the other line to make an upside down V shape.
- Jump from line to line.

Pre-Activity Prep

Place a line of tape on the ground.

Other Notes

Although this seems like a simple activity, it really is one that toddlers love!

PAPER PLATE RING TOSS

Materials Needed

- paper plates
- scissors
- paint
- paintbrushes
- cardboard tubes
- glue

Pre-Activity Prep

Paint the paper plates. When they are dry, cut the centers out of the plates to make rings. Glue one end of the cardboard tube to a white paper plate.

Ways to Play

- Set the cardboard tube and plate upright and toss the rings over the cardboard tube; when your child can make the toss consistently, start moving them back to further distances! If your child struggles with the tossing motion at first, you can start by simply sliding the rings onto the tube, then progress by having them hold the rings over the tube and then drop them straight down.

GROSS MOTOR

Materials Needed

- rhythm scarves

Ways to Play

- Scrunch the scarf into a ball, throw it in the air and try to catch it.
- Toss the scarf in the air and touch your hand to the opposite shoulder.
- Sit directly behind your toddler and pass the scarf to him on the left side and then have him rotate his torso and pass it back to you on the right side.

Other Notes

Rhythm scarves are an awesome way for children to work on crossing the midline. Crossing the body midline is the ability to reach across the middle of the body with the arms and legs crossing over to the opposite side. This is an important developmental skill because it helps with hand-eye coordination and everyday tasks such as writing and hitting a ball with a bat.

G R O S S M O T O R

OTHER GROSS MOTOR IDEAS

There are lots of ways to work on gross motor skills and many of these ideas don't require detailed instructions. Here are 10 simple ideas:

1. Walking backwards
2. Rolling balls
3. Climbing a low stool
4. Throwing and catching balls
5. Pushing a cardboard box
6. Rolling their body (like a log)
7. Jumping with 2 feet
8. Climbing the stairs or ladder to a slide
9. Walking across a low balance beam
10. Stretching with yoga poses

Fine Motor Skills

Fine motor skills are the actions that are performed using the hands, fingers and wrists. Like gross motor skills, these skills are very important to work on. Your child practices using fine motor skills while pinching a toy, holding a pencil, using a pair of scissors, or lacing their shoes. Fine motor skills develop through lots of practice. Having strong fine motor skills will prepare your child for holding a pencil and learning to write.

Once your child starts school, good control of the hand muscles will help your child learn handwriting with ease. This is a huge confidence booster and will help your child feel more positive about learning.

In order for fine motor skills to develop, there are four essential bases that need to be in place.

1. **Postural Control**—The ability for the muscles of the shoulders and trunk to stabilize the arms, so the fingers are free to move.

2. **Touch Perception**—The ability for the brain to receive good feedback from what your fingers are doing and touching.

3. **Bilateral Coordination**—The ability to use both sides of the body together in a coordinated way.

4. **Hand Function**—The ability for the muscles of the hand to work together in order to control pencils, scissors, or other small objects.

While the 25 fine motor ideas in this book are fun play activities, they can make a big impact on fine motor skills.

rials Needed

ers

Ways to Play

- Poke the pipe cleaners into the holes of the colander.
- Bend the pipe cleaners and continue to poke them into the holes.

d
r
g
:
d

d
d

e

g

rials Needed

POM P

Materials Needed

- pom poms
- paper towel tube

Pre-Activity Prep

- Tape a paper towel tube to the wall.

Ways to

- Drop pom poms in t
  tube and watch then
  bottom.
- Place two tubes on t
  race the pom poms.
- To make this more s
  pipes instead. Arran
  using PVC pipes and
  gun or zip ties to se
  pegboard.

COTTON BALL PUSH

Materials Needed

- empty coffee creamer bottle
- cotton balls

Ways to Play

- Push the cotton balls into the bottle.
- Shake the bottle with the cotton balls in it.
- Dump the cotton balls out and fill it again!

PIPE CLEANER DROP

Materials Needed

- empty chip can
- 4 colors of pipe cleaners
- 4 white reinforcement circle labels
- 4 markers
- X-Acto knife or hole punch
- paper or felt

Ways to Play

- Poke the pipe cleaners through the holes.
- Match the pipe cleaners to the correct color.

Pre-Activity Prep

Cover the can with paper or a piece of felt. Take the lid and make 4 holes in it. Color the white reinforcement circle labels to match the pipe cleaner colors. Then place the colored circles onto the holes. Place the lid back on the can.

Other Notes

You can also cut the pipe cleaners to a smaller size so that you can fit more of them in the can.

TAPE PULLING

FINE MOTOR

Materials Needed

- masking tape

Pre-Activity Prep

Place lines of tape on a table.

Ways to Play

- Pull up the tape from the table.
- Use colored tape and have your child practice naming the colors while pulling the tape up.

Other Notes

This is such a simple activity, but your toddler will love it! It can be tricky to find a corner to pull up, but it's fun pulling it up and hearing the sound it makes.

Make sure to test the table or floor to be sure it doesn't damage them.

Materials Needed

- scrap paper, magazines, or junk mail

Ways to Play

- Simply tear the paper into pieces.

Other Notes

While tearing the paper, the finge form into the "pencil grip". This activ is a great way to prepare children 1 handwriting.

Tearing leads to the ability to do sk like opening bags of shredded chee: tearing lettuce leafs, and using a zipp

als Needed

lock

F I N E   M O T O R

Ways to Play

- Use the hammer to tap the golf tees into the Styrofoam block.
- Place X's around the Styrofoam and have your child hammer the golf tees in those spots.
- To make the activity a little easier, poke the golf tees in the Styrofoam first and hold the golf tees in place while your child hammers them in.

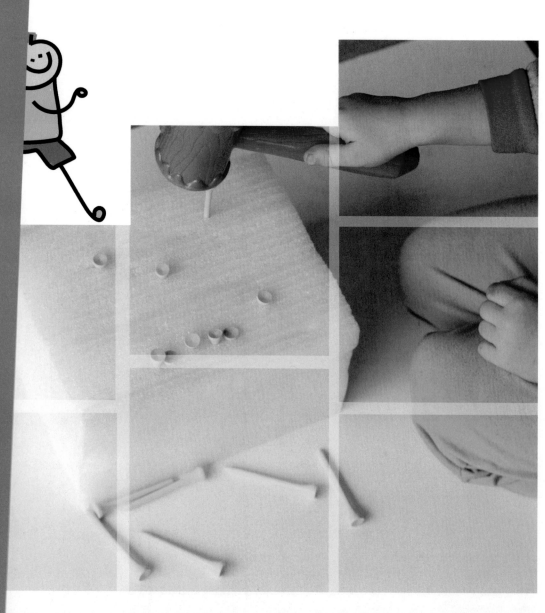

Materials Needed

- long piece of wide ribbon
- colored felt
- 1 large button
- scissors
- needle & thread

Pre-Activity Prep

Cut felt into 3 inch squares. Fold the square felt pieces in half and make a small slit in the middle. Sew the button on one end of the ribbon.

Ways to Play

- Slip one square of felt onto the button snake. Slide it all the way to the bottom until it reaches the button. Keep adding felt to the button snake until it is full.

FINE MOTOR

POOL NOODLE THREADING

Materials Needed

- 2 feet of rope
- serrated knife
- pool noodle

Ways to Play

- Thread the pool noodle pieces onto the piece of string. Continue adding noodle pieces until the rope is full.
- Make a pattern with different colored pool noodle pieces.
- Make a pool noodle necklace when the rope is filled.

Pre-Activity Prep

- Cut up the pool noodle into pieces using a knife. Tie a large knot on one end of the rope.

F I N E

M O T O R

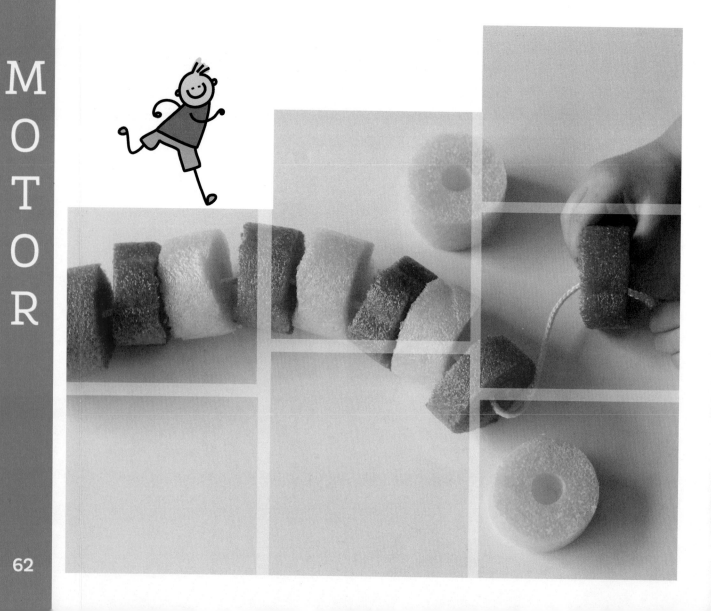

Materials Needed

- sponges
- bin with water

Pre-Activity Prep

Cut the sponges into shapes or pieces.

Ways to Play

- Place the sponges into a bin with some water.
- Squeeze the sponges and wring out the water.
- Transfer water from one bin to another by squeezing the sponges.
- Talk about the colors and shapes of the sponges as you play.

FINE MOTOR

FINE MOTOR

Materials Needed

- play dough
- pipe cleaners
- beads

Ways to Play

- Slide beads down the pipe cleaner.
- Create patterns with the beads.
- After the pipe cleaner is full, make it into a bracelet by wrapping it around your wrist and twisting the ends together.

Pre-Activity Prep

Roll play dough into a ball and poke a pipe cleaner into it.

Other Notes

Only do this activity with children who do not put items in their mouths.

18-24 **24-36**

Materials Needed

- old CDs
- disc spindle

Ways to Play

- Place the individual CDs onto the disc spindle.
- To make it harder, use tongs or tweezers to place the CDs onto the disc spindle.

FINE MOTOR

FINE MOTOR

Materials Needed

- empty parmesan container
- pipe cleaners

Ways to Play

- Drop the pipe cleaner pieces into the parmesan container.
- Once all the pipe cleaner pieces are in the container, shake them out and fill it again!

Pre-Activity Prep

Cut up the pipe cleaners into 2-inch pieces.

CORK DROP

Materials Needed

- corks
- plastic jug

Other Notes

As your toddler drops in corks, he will discover the texture, size, and shape of the corks. While he's strengthening his fine motor skills, he'll also work on hand-eye coordination.

Ways to Play

- Place a bowl with corks next to an empty plastic jug. Individually drop the corks into the jug until all the corks are gone!

FINE MOTOR

FINE MOTOR

Materials Needed

- spray bottle
- water
- plastic bin
- rubber ducks (or objects that float)

Ways to Play

- Spray the bottle and aim for the rubber ducks.
- Try to squirt the ducks from one side of the bin to the other side.
- Race against another child to see which duck reaches the other side faster.

Pre-Activity Prep

Fill the bin with a few inches of water and place the rubber ducks into the bin.

Other Notes

Using a spray bottle is a difficult fine motor activity, so don't be discouraged if your child is not able to do it the first time you try this activity.

Materials Needed

- play dough
- spaghetti noodles (uncooked)
- Cheerios

Pre-Activity Prep

Roll play dough into a ball and poke uncooked spaghetti noodles into it.

Ways to Play

- Have the child thread Cheerios onto the spaghetti noodle.
- See if they can get the Cheerios all the way to the top before the noodle breaks!
- Count the Cheerios while threading them.
- If you use colored Cheerios, sort the cereal by color or make patterns.

FINE MOTOR

DON'T DROP THE POM POM!

Materials Needed

- 2 bowls
- medium-sized pom poms
- tongs

Ways to Play

- Set out two bowls and fill one with pom poms. Pick up the pom poms using tongs and transfer them to another bowl. Try to not drop the pom poms while you're moving them.
- Pick up the pom poms and transfer them to a container with a lid that has a hole in it. See if they can drop the pom poms through the hole without using their fingers.
- Use tweezers if the tongs are too easy for your child.
- Sort the pom poms by colors.

FINE MOTOR

Materials Needed

- squeeze bottle with warm water
- frozen block of ice with items inside of it
- plastic bin

Pre-Activity Prep

Fill a bowl with water and put items inside of it, such as sequins, beads, or small plastic toys. Place in the freezer until it forms to solid ice.

Ways to Play

- Squeeze the bottle of warm water onto the block of ice.
- Dig the items out of the ice once it starts to melt.
- Feel the ice and talk about how it feels: cold, slippery, wet, etc.

FINE MOTOR

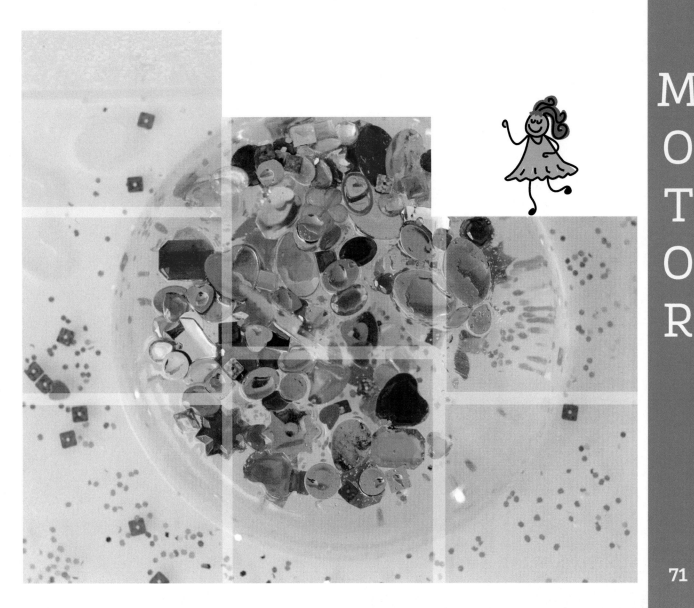

Q-TIP DROP

Materials Needed

- Q-tips
- canister
- drill

Ways to Play

- Drop the Q-tips into the holes and fill the canister.
- Shake the canister and listen to how it sounds when it contains Q-tips.

Pre-Activity Prep

Drill holes into the lid of the canister.

FINE MOTOR

Materials Needed

- Velcro strips
- pictures

Pre-Activity Prep

Place Velcro strips on a sturdy surface, such as a table or a wall. Place the other side of the Velcro strip onto the backside of a picture. Place the pictures onto the Velcro.

Ways to Play

- Have your toddler look at the pictures and pull them down from the Velcro. Also have them place the pictures back onto the Velcro.
- Put pictures up of familiar faces (such as family members) and talk about their names to work on verbal skills.
- Put pictures up of animals, colors, or shapes and have your toddler practice identifying them.

FINE MOTOR

COTTON BALL SMASH

Materials Needed

- 1 cup of flour
- 1 cup of water
- whisk
- bowls
- food coloring
- tin foil
- baking sheet
- cotton balls
- toy hammer
- oven

Ways to Play

- Smash the baked cotton balls with the toy hammer.
- Squeeze the cotton balls to make them crunch.

Pre-Activity Prep

Line a baking sheet with tin foil. Mix the cup of flour with a cup or water and mix with a whisk. Add in food coloring. Dip cotton balls into the mixture and lay them onto the cookie sheet. Bake in the oven at 300 degrees Fahrenheit for 45 minutes.

Other Notes

This activity is great for working on hand-eye coordination.

FINE MOTOR

18-24 | 24-36

Materials Needed

- pool noodle
- pom poms
- tongs (optional)

Pre-Activity Prep

Cut up a pool noodle into pieces using a serrated knife. Place the cut up pool noodle pieces onto a tray with a bowl of pom poms next to it.

Ways to Play

- Push a pom pom through the center of each pool noodle piece to make it look like a flower.
- Talk about the names of the colors as you put a pom pom inside the hole.
- Make a pattern with the colors.
- Pop the pom poms out of the pool noodle pieces when all of them have been filled.

FINE MOTOR

FINE MOTOR

Materials Needed

- play dough
- kid scissors

Ways to Play

- Use kid scissors to cut the play dough snakes into pieces.

Pre-Activity Prep

Roll the play dough into snakes.

Other Notes

This is the ideal scissor grasp: the thumb through one hole and the middle finger through the other hole, and the index finger resting on the outside of the scissors. It forms a tripod, which builds the foundation for handwriting.

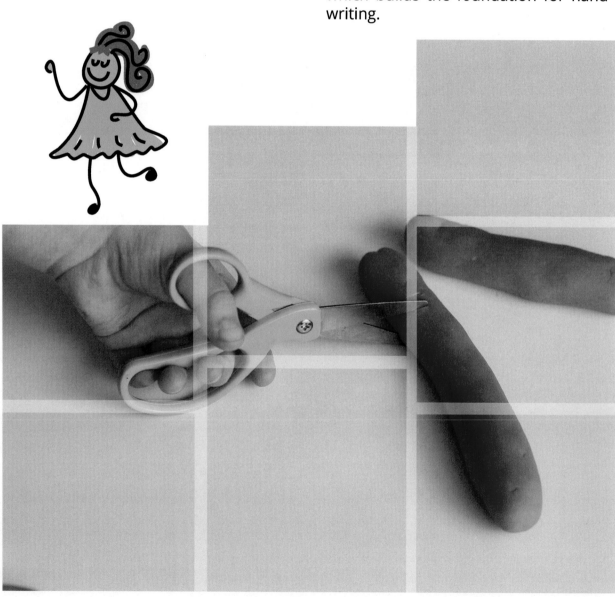

CRAZY STRAW THREADING

Materials Needed

- crazy straw
- foam sheets

Pre-Activity Prep

Cut out shapes from foam sheets.

Ways to Play

- Thread the crazy straw through the shapes.
- Make patterns with the shapes and colors on the straw.
- Time your child to see how quickly they can thread the straw through the shapes.

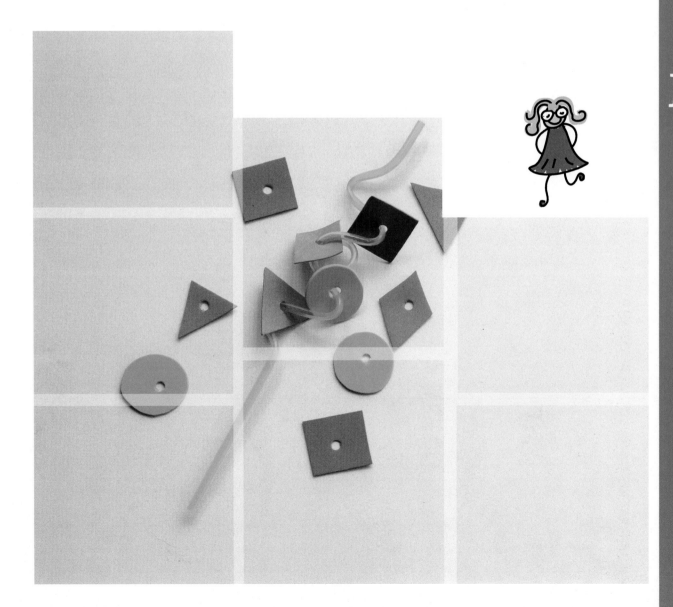

FINE MOTOR

DANDELION POKE

Materials Needed

- colander
- dandelions

Other Notes

Poking the stem through the holes can be a hard skill. Teach toddlers to keep their fingers near the base of the stem so it's easier to place them into the holes. This activity allows children to practice the pencil grip hold, which is great for handwriting.

Ways to Play

- Have the child pick dandelions or other flowers.
- Poke the flower stems through the holes in the colander.

78

Art Activities

C an toddlers really do art activities? Yes, they can! And trust me, they will love doing these 15 art activities. It's important to allow time for the child to develop an interest in art. The more exposure to art they have, the more time they have for creativity and imagination to develop.

Toddlers work on fine motor skills while doing art. Whether it's holding a paintbrush or using the pincer grasp to hold tissue paper squares, they are building up strength in their fingers, wrists, and hands.

When doing art activities with toddlers, it's important to keep these things in mind:

- Don't expect toddlers to create art or crafts that look polished.

- There should be an emphasis on the process of creating art, rather than an end product.

- Expect a short attention span with toddlers. They may start a project and then come back to it another day.

- Remember that toddlers love to put items in their mouth, so use taste-safe or nontoxic products.

A lot of the art activities in this book involve paint. My favorite paint to use is Crayola Washable Tempera Paint. We buy the big bottles and they last a long time. If you want a little bit thicker paint, I recommend using Crayola Washable Finger Paint. These work well for activities with stamping. While I suggest using food coloring to create colors, you can also use Coloration Liquid Watercolors. There are so many great colors and they last much longer.

The most important thing to remember while creating art with toddlers is that it is a process and the goal is not to create masterpieces, but to have fun with the activities.

A R T   A C T I V I T I E S

Materials Needed

- washable paint
- large piece of paper
- tape
- vehicles

Pre-Activity Prep

Tape paper onto the table.

Ways to Play

- Dip the vehicles into the paint and roll them across the paper.
- Try different types of vehicles: cars, trucks, trains, motorcycles, etc.
- Make designs around the paper or even create a race track!

SIDEWALK PAINT

Materials Needed

- 1 cup cornstarch
- 1 cup water
- food coloring
- muffin tin
- paintbrushes

Ways to Play

- Paint the sidewalk using paintbrushes.

Pre-Activity Prep

Mix the cornstarch with the water. Pour the mixture into a muffin tin. Add 1-2 drops of food coloring and mix.

Other Notes

The sidewalk paint will wash off with water.

COTTON BALL PAINTING

18-24 24-36

Materials Needed

- cotton balls
- clothespins
- paint
- paper

Ways to Play

- Dip the cotton ball into paint and stamp, slide, or swirl it to make neat designs on the piece of paper.

Pre-Activity Prep

Attach the clothespins to the cotton balls.

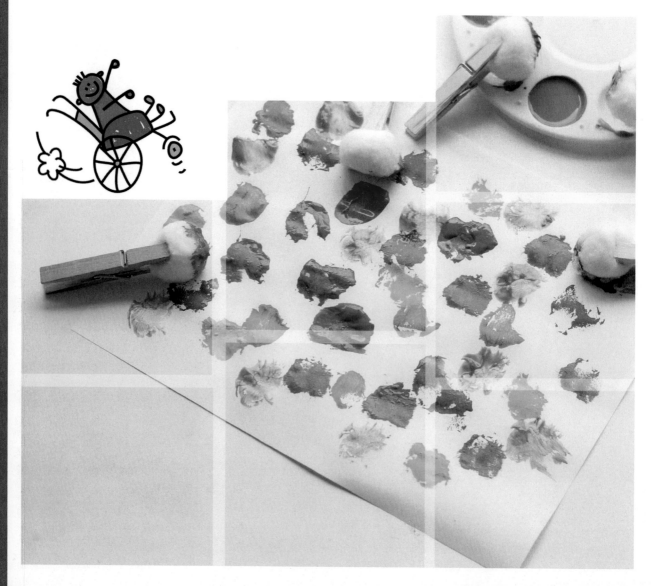

12-18 **18-24** **24-36**

Materials Needed

- vanilla or plain yogurt
- food coloring (optional)
- muffin tin or bowls
- paintbrushes
- paper

Ways to Play

- Use paintbrushes or fingers to paint a design onto a piece of paper.

Pre-Activity Prep

Pour the yogurt into a muffin tin and mix in food coloring.

Other Notes

This recipe is for one-time use. Please dispose of it after the activity is done.

ICE CUBE PAINTING

| | 18-24 | 24-36 |

Materials Needed

- ice cube tray
- water
- food coloring
- toothpicks or popsicle sticks
- paper

Ways to Play

- Hold the toothpicks and slide the cube across the paper to make designs. The art will look similar to watercolor paint.

Pre-Activity Prep

Add water to an ice cube tray. Place 1-2 drops of food coloring into each section of the tray and mix. Place in the freezer for 20 minutes. Add a toothpick to the cubes and then place in the freezer until frozen solid.

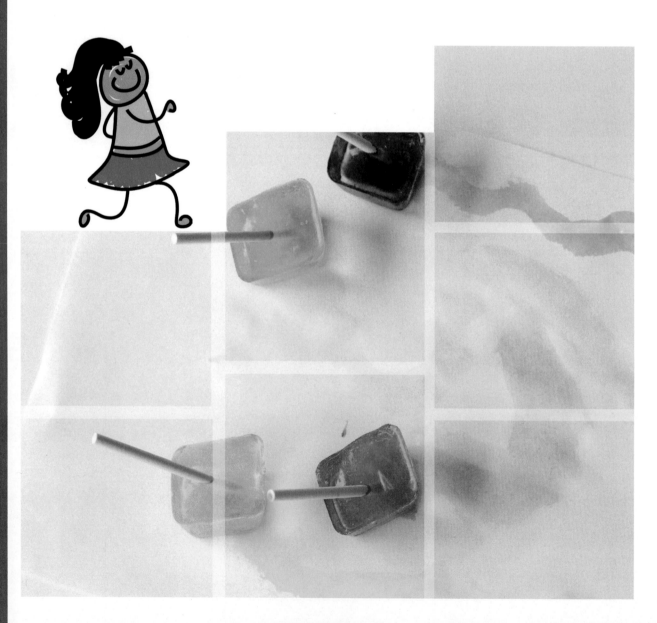

Materials Needed

- sponges
- paint
- paper

Ways to Play

- Dip the sponge into paint and stamp it around the piece of paper.
- Use various colors and show children how two primary colors mixed together can create another color.

SOAP FOAM PAINTING

Materials Needed

- squeeze bottles
- 1/4 cup water
- 2 tablespoons dish soap
- food coloring
- food processor or blender
- sidewalk

Ways to Play

- Squeeze the bottles onto the sidewalk to create pictures and designs.

Pre-Activity Prep

Place the dish soap, water, and a few drops of food coloring inside of the food processor or blender. Turn it on for a minute or two (until the soap foam rises to the top). Scoop out the soap foam and put it in a squeeze bottle. Repeat the recipe to make other colors.

Other Notes

Use the soap foam right away to keep it foamy. If the foam goes down, either shake the bottle or put it back into the blender for a minute.

STAMPING WITH APPLES

Materials Needed

- apples
- paint
- paper

Ways to Play

- Dip the apple into the paint and stamp around the piece of paper.
- Create designs or make patterns with colors.
- Talk about the different colors or even show how two primary colors mixed together can make another color.

Pre-Activity Prep

Cut an apple in half and then cut two sections out to create handles in the apple.

CONTACT PAPER COLLAGE

Materials Needed

- contact paper
- tape
- materials to fill the collage: pom poms, sequins, tissue paper squares, pipe cleaner pieces, foam shapes, etc.

Ways to Play

- Create designs on the contact paper using various materials.

Pre-Activity Prep

Tape the edges of contact paper onto a table, making sure the sticky part is facing up.

PAINTING ON FOIL

Materials Needed

- aluminum foil
- paint

Ways to Play

- Paint designs onto the foil.
- Use different types of paint: tempera paint, finger paint, yogurt paint, shaving cream, or puffy paint.

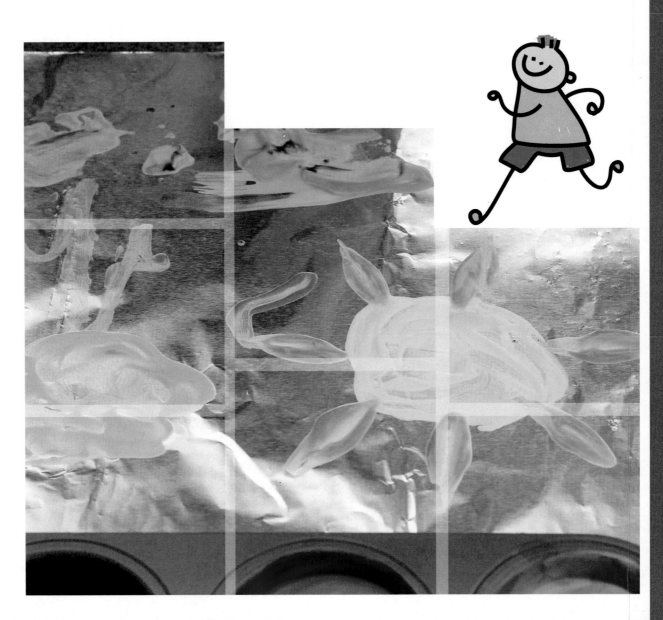

ART ACTIVITIES

PUFFY PAINT

Materials Needed

- squeeze bottles
- 1 cup flour
- 3 teaspoons baking soda
- 1 teaspoon salt
- 1-1/4 cup water
- food coloring
- paper

Pre-Activity Prep

Mix the flour, baking soda, and salt together. Gradually add water. Continue adding water until the mixture looks like pancake batter, then mix in your color. Pour into a squeeze bottle.

Ways to Play

- Squeeze the puffy paint onto the piece of paper, making designs. Let it air dry, or place it in the microwave for 30 seconds.

Other Notes

The puffy paint should be discarded after 5 days.

TISSUE PAPER COLLAGE

Materials Needed

- tissue paper
- contact paper

Pre-Activity Prep

Cut the tissue paper into 2-inch squares.

Ways to Play

- Place the tissue paper pieces onto the contact paper. Since the contact paper is sticky, the pieces will stay in place.
- Create a design with the colored tissue paper.
- Cut out a shape with the contact paper (such as a heart) and fill it in with tissue paper.

Other Notes

To preserve this piece of art, seal it together with another piece of contact paper on top.

ART ACTIVITIES

Materials Needed

- small plastic container or tissue box
- 3 or more rubber bands
- paint
- piece of paper

Ways to Play

- Flick the rubber bands to make paint splatter onto the piece of paper.
- If you run out of paint, add more to the rubber bands.

Pre-Activity Prep

Wrap rubber bands around the container. Place a piece of paper underneath the rubber bands. Use your finger to smear paint onto the rubber bands.

Other Notes

This can splatter paint on your clothing, so make sure to wear paint clothes or an art smock.

COOKIE CUTTER STAMPING

Materials Needed

- paint
- cookie cutters
- paper

Ways to Play

- Dip the cookie cutter into paint and stamp it onto a piece of paper.
- Try this activity with paper towel rolls, too! You can make circles or bend it to look like a heart.

PAINTING WITH DANDELIONS

18-24 **24-36**

Materials Needed

- dandelions (or another flower)
- paint
- paper

Ways to Play

- Dip the dandelion into the paint and then stamp them onto a piece of paper.
- Create designs or make patterns with the dandelions.

Pre-Activity Prep

Gather dandelions or other flowers from outside.

Mess-Free Activities

In this toddler activity book, you're probably noticing a trend; a lot of these activities create a mess. Your initial thought may be "I don't want to ever try that activity because it's just too messy!" Before you say that, let me just share a few reasons why I believe messy play is important!

1. These activities allow young children to explore using their senses. Children learn primarily through play, so combining their need to play and their need to explore often results in a mess. So much learning happens through these types of activities!

2. Having rich texture activities helps children refine their sense of touch. They experience what different materials feel like. Messy play materials should include different textures (rough, smooth, wet, dry) and temperatures (cold, warm).

3. Children develop stronger language skills. How can a child describe what "slimy" means if he has never touched anything "slimy"?

4. They can be creative! These play activities encourage children to explore and be imaginative.

5. Messy play activities create a better relationship with the parent! If a mess is always discouraged, it can lead to a stressful relationship between the parent and child. They may also avoid messy play in the future and can lead to a diminished sense of touch and could limit cognitive development.

While messy play activities are important to do with children, we also need activities that are mess-free. These ideas come in handy when we need our house to stay picked up or a quiet activity to keep children busy. Here are my 10 favorite ways to keep toddlers busy, without creating a big mess!

PAINT IN A BAG

Materials Needed

- gallon sized Ziploc bag
- paint
- tape

Ways to Play

- Use fingers to feel the paint and mix the colors together.
- Create designs with the paint or just enjoy how it feels to swirl the paint around with your fingers.

Pre-Activity Prep

Squirt paint inside of a bag and tape it to the table or window.

Other Notes

If you're worried about the bag opening up, place another bag around it.

MESS FREE

STUFFED ANIMAL BATH

Materials Needed

- bathtub
- stuffed animals

Ways to Play

- Place lots of stuffed animals into a dry bathtub.
- Let the child use their imagination to play with the stuffed animals.
- Here are some ideas for playing: pretend to be on a boat, act like a veterinarian taking care of the animals, or pretend to be flying on an airplane.

MESS FREE

CAR WASH STATION

Materials Needed

- sink of water
- soap or shaving cream
- squeeze or spray bottles
- towels
- cars

Ways to Play

- Pretend to be at a car wash and the job is to clean the dirty cars. Have your child clean the cars with soap, water, and dry them off with a towel.

Pre-Activity Prep

Fill the sink with water and place soap and towels next to the sink.

Other Notes

Dramatic play is an important activity for little ones to do. It helps them use their imagination to act out real-world tasks.

MESS FREE

TOWER BUILDING WITH RECYCLABLES

Materials Needed

- empty food boxes

Pre-Activity Prep

Tape the open sides of the boxes down.

Ways to Play

- Stack food boxes to build towers.
- Knock them down and build them again!

MESS FREE

SENSORY BALLOON ANIMALS

Materials Needed

- balloons
- funnel
- materials to fill the balloons: rice, beans, popcorn kernels, etc.
- black permanent marker

Pre-Activity Prep

Attach a funnel to the opening on the balloon. Fill the balloon with rice, beans, or popcorn kernels. Tie the balloon shut. Draw a face of an animal onto the balloon, such as a bee, ladybug, mouse, lion, or cat.

Ways to Play

- Squeeze the balloons and talk about how they feel.
- Throw and catch the balloon animals.
- Place a basket on one side of the room and practice throwing them into the basket.
- Use imaginary play to play with the balloon animals.

M E S S   F R E E

SPONGE BUILDING

Materials Needed

- 10 or more sponges

Ways to Play

- Use the sponge pieces to build designs.

Pre-Activity Prep

Cut the sponges into shapes, such as rectangles, squares, circles, hearts, or triangles.

Other Notes

After playing, store them in a Ziploc bag. Add a small amount of water to the bag to keep the sponges from drying up.

MESS FREE

PAINT WITH WATER

18-24   24-36

Materials Needed

- bucket of water
- paintbrushes or rollers
- sidewalk

Ways to Play

- Paint the sidewalk with water using paintbrushes or roller brushes.
- Create designs with the water.
- Observe how quickly the sun dries up the water!

MESS FREE

HOMEMADE PUZZLES WITH RECYCLABLES

Materials Needed

- empty food boxes

Ways to Play

- Arrange the pieces and put them together to look like the front of the box.

Pre-Activity Prep

Cut out the front of the box and cut it into large pieces, like a puzzle.

VELCRO STICKS

Materials Needed

- craft sticks
- circle Velcro tabs

Ways to Play

- Match the Velcro on the craft sticks to other sticks to form shapes, letters, and other designs.
- Talk about the colors of the sticks, the shapes you design with the sticks, and the sound you hear when you pull the sticks apart.

Pre-Activity Prep

Place Velcro tabs on both ends of the craft sticks.

MESS FREE

Materials Needed

- cardboard box lid
- black paint
- yellow paint
- vehicles

Ways to Play

- Use vehicles to drive along the track.
- Bring it into the car to keep kids busy on a road trip.

Pre-Activity Prep

Paint a racetrack using black paint onto the cardboard box lid. Add yellow lines to make it look like a road.

M
E
S
S

F
R
E
E

ABOUT THE AUTHOR

Angela is a mom to 3 boys, wife to an amazing man, lover of the Midwest, coffee enthusiast, and daughter of a loving God. She is the writer and creator at TeachingMama.org, where she shares learning activities for babies, toddlers, and preschoolers. Angela is also the author of *The Preschool Journey*, a 26-week hands-on preschool curriculum. She is a former teacher and has a bachelor's degree in Elementary Education. Angela has a passion for educating children, as well as helping parents of little ones thrive during the early childhood years.

CONNECT WITH HER AT:

Facebook @TeachingMamaBlog

Twitter @TeachingMama_

Instagram @angelateachingmama

Pinterest @angelathayer

Made in the USA
San Bernardino, CA
07 August 2016